Little Mitchie

LET'S LOOK INSIDE A SPORTS CAR

LET'S LOOK INSIDE: VEHICLES

PAUL ZACHARY

CREATING YOUNG NONFICTION READERS

Little Mitchie books spark curiosity and support early nonfiction reading for students in Grades 2-3. Designed to build vocabulary, support second language learners, and prepare readers for middle-grade content, each book includes helpful tips for parents and educators to build confidence and deepen understanding of the world.

TIPS FOR READING NONFICTION WITH BEGINNING READERS

Talk about Nonfiction

Begin by explaining that nonfiction books give us information that is true. The book will be organized around a specific topic or idea, and we may learn new facts through reading.

Look at the Parts

Most nonfiction books have helpful features. Our *Little Mitchie* titles include color photographs and graphic aids, a table of contents, a glossary, and an index. Share the purpose of these features with your reader.

Color Photos and Graphic Aids

A lot of information can be found by "reading" photos, charts, maps, and other graphic aids found within nonfiction texts. Help your reader learn more about the different ways information can be displayed.

Table of Contents

Located at the front of the book, this list shows the big ideas within the text and the page numbers where they can be found.

Glossary

Located at the back of the book, the glossary defines key words and phrases that are related to the topic. These words and phrases can be found in the text in colored type.

Index

Located at the back of the book, an index is an alphabetical list of topics and the page numbers where they can be found.

With a little help and guidance about reading nonfiction, you can feel good about introducing a young reader to the world of *Little Mitchie* nonfiction books.

Little Mitchie is an imprint of:

Mitchell Lane
PUBLISHERS

2001 SW 31st Avenue
Hallandale, FL 33009
mitchelllanepub.com

First Edition, 2027.

Author: Paul Zachary
Designer: Rhea Magaro
Editor: Tricia Hoffman

Library of Congress Cataloging-in-Publication Data
Title: Let's Look Inside a Sports Car / by Paul Zachary.

Description: Hallandale, FL :
Mitchell Lane Publishers, [2027]

Identifiers:
ISBN 979-8-89260-880-0 (library bound)
ISBN 979-8-90145-050-5 (paperback)
ISBN 979-8-89260-983-8 (eBook)

Library of Congress Control Number: 2026930137

Photo credits: Alamy: Ambrosiniv, 6; Maksim Kostenko, 14; Shutterstock: Poetra.RH, 1, 3, 4, 8, 17; Brandon Woyshnis, 5; Gorodenkoff, 9; jhxfilm, 10; JoshBryan, 12; JustPhotos22, 13; Fotokon, 16; witaker, 19; Jakub Sisulak, 21; MOUTASEM PHOTOGRAPHY, 22

TABLE OF CONTENTS

Chapter One

ZOOM! HERE IT COMES!

Vroom! Vroom! Here comes a shiny red sports car, speeding down the road like a rocket! It zooms past trees, around corners, and over rolling hills.

FAST FACT

Many sports cars are painted bright colors like red, yellow, or orange so other drivers can easily see them on the road.

FAST FACT

Some sports cars have special doors that open upward instead of sideways!

Have you ever wondered what the inside of a sports car is like? Let's open the door and take a look!

Chapter Two

IN THE DRIVER'S SEAT

Slide into the driver's seat. It sits low to the ground and feels super snug. The **bucket seat** hugs the driver like a racing suit, keeping them steady during fast turns.

FAST FACT

Car makers test sports cars in special rooms called wind tunnels to see how air moves around the car.

ENGINE
START
STOP

The **steering wheel** is small and sporty. Push the big red button to start the car. The **engine** roars to life!

The **dashboard** glows with colorful lights and **digital** screens. One display shows how fast you're going—and sports cars can go fast!

FAST FACT

Everything inside the car is made for speed, comfort, and fun!

There is a **gear shift** in the middle of the car. It looks a little like a joystick. Drivers move the gear shift to change gears. This helps the car go faster, slower, or even backward.

ALIEN
ALIEN
Pelying

Chapter Three

READY, SET, DRIVE!

Don't forget the sound system—music plays loud and clear through big speakers. You can sing along while the wind whooshes past your window!

There's not much room in the **trunk**. Sports cars are made to be light and fast, not heavy and full.

Look up! Some sports cars are **convertibles**, and with the push of a button, the top folds back. Now you can feel the sun on your face and the breeze in your hair while you cruise down the road.

FAST FACT

Sports cars are shaped to cut through the air. This helps them go faster and ride smoother!

Chapter Four

BUILT FOR SPEED

Sports cars are built for speed, style, and fun, and now you know what's inside one—a roaring engine, a glowing dashboard, and a driver ready to zoom! The next time you see a sports car drive by, listen for the *vroom*!

A LOOK INSIDE

GLOSSARY

bucket seat (buhk-it seet) a deep car seat shaped to hold one person comfortably

convertible (kuhn-vur-tuh-buhl) a car with a top that can be put down

dashboard (dash-bord) the instrument panel in front of the driver that shows speed and other information

digital (dij-i-tuhl) numbers or information shown on a screen instead of a dial

engine (en-jin) the part of a car that makes it move

gear shift (geer shift) a stick the driver moves to change gears

steering wheel (steer-ing weel) the wheel the driver turns to steer the car

trunk (truhngk) the storage space in the back of a car

FURTHER READING

Gish, Ashley. *Sports Cars.* The Creative Company, 2021.

James, Ryan. *Sports Cars.* Crabtree Publishing, 2023.

ON THE INTERNET

Sports Car Facts for Kids

https://kids.kiddle.co/Sportscar

Easy-to-read basics about what a sports car is, what it's like inside, and what makes it special. Great for simple sports car facts in a kid-friendly language.

Automobile Racing

https://kids.britannica.com/kids/article/automobile-racing/442824

Britannica Kids explains the history of automobile racing and rallies.

INDEX